SELF-LOVE SYMPHONY

8 RESONANT NOTES OF SELF-LOVE

PIYUSH SINGH

Made with ♥ on the Notion Press Platform
www.notionpress.com

Me with My Parents

Dedicated to the memory of my beloved mother, Your love, guidance, and unwavering support inspired me to chase my dreams, even when the world seemed darkest. Your kindness, generosity, and compassion taught me the true meaning of selflessness and empathy. Your strength and resilience in adversity showed me that I could overcome any obstacle.

Though you may no longer be with me physically, your spirit lives on in every word, every sentence, and every page of this book. I hope it makes you proud.

To my readers, I share this dedication with you, hoping that it may inspire you to hold your loved ones close, cherish every moment, and never take anything for granted. May my mother's memory be a blessing to us all.

Contents

Preface   vii

Acknowledgements   ix

Prologue   xi

1. Discovering The Beauty Within   1

2. Letting Go Of Perfection   5

3. Accepting Your Flaws   9

4. Positive Changes, One Step At A Time   15

5. Practicing Gratitude   21

6. Surrounding Yourself With Positivity   28

7. The Power Of Self-Care   36

8. Embracing Your Journey   43

About the Author   49

Afterword   51

Preface

In this chaotic world, where we often find ourselves lost in the midst of expectations and societal pressures, it's easy to forget the most important person in our lives - ourselves. Self-love is not just a feeling, but a choice. A choice to accept ourselves with all our flaws and imperfections, to embrace our uniqueness, and to love ourselves unconditionally.

"Self-love Symphony" is a journey of self-discovery, a reminder that we are enough, just as we are. Through these pages, I invite you to join me on a path of self-love, self-acceptance, and self-empowerment. Let us break free from the chains of negativity and self-doubt, and let us learn to love ourselves with all our hearts.

In this book, I share my personal experiences, insights, and lessons learned on my own journey of self-love. I hope that my story will inspire and motivate you to embark on your own journey of self-discovery and self-love.

So, let us begin this symphony of self-love, and let the music of our hearts guide us towards a life of love, acceptance, and empowerment.

Acknowledgements

I am grateful to the following individuals who have played a significant role in the creation of this book:

To my loving family (my **father**,my **step mom**,my brothers **Pratik & Priyanshu** and also my loving sister **Priya**), who have supported me unconditionally throughout this journey. Your love and encouragement mean the world to me.

To my dear friends (*Anam,Anveshika,Ankita,Tanu,Divyendra,Deepak,Siddharth & Vishnu*), who have been my pillars of strength, my confidants, and my partners in crime. Thank you for being my sounding board, my reality check, and my constant source of inspiration.

To my teachers (<u>**Rajesh Guruji,Vijayalaxmi Didiji,Amitabh Guruji,Anuj Sir,Ankit Awasthi Sir,Vijay Agrawal Sir,Ripusudan Sir**</u>)I'm grateful for your guidance, wisdom, and patience, which have transformed my life. Your teachings have not only enlightened me academically but also instilled valuable life lessons. You've inspired me to strive for excellence and shaped me into the person I am today. Thank you for your tireless efforts, unwavering support, and dedication to nurturing young minds.

To my **Mahadev** (Lord Shiva). He supported me when the world did not belive in me. He kept blessings me during my difficult time.

And to those who have chosen to **leave my life**, I thank you too. Your departure has taught me the value of self-love, self-worth, and the importance of setting boundaries. Your selfishness has been a catalyst for my growth, and for that, I am eternally grateful.

To everyone who has **touched my life** in some way, I thank you for being a part of my journey. Your presence, absence, love, and indifference have all contributed to the person I am today, and for that, I am thankful.

This book is a testament to the power of self-love and resilience. May it inspire you to love yourself unconditionally, just as I have learned to do.

Prologue

"In the grand orchestra of life, there is one instrument that often remains silent - the voice of self-love. We are taught to prioritize others, to put their needs before our own, and to seek validation from external sources. But what happens when the music of self-doubt, fear, and criticism fills our minds? What happens when we forget to love ourselves?

This book is an invitation to awaken the instrument of self-love within you. To tune into its gentle whispers, to amplify its harmonies, and to let its symphony guide you towards a life of purpose, joy, and fulfillment.

In the following pages, we'll explore the 8 resonant notes of self-love - notes that will help you silence the noise of self-doubt, and harmonize your heart, mind, and soul. Get ready to embark on a journey of transformation, one that will awaken the love, light, and music within you."

CHAPTER ONE

Discovering the Beauty Within

"Welcome, dear reader, to a journey that has the potential to transform your life in ways you may have never imagined. Today, we embark on a path that leads to one of the most valuable gifts you can ever offer yourself: self-love. This journey isn't about vanity or self-indulgence; it's about cultivating a deep, authentic appreciation for who you are, inside and out."

You might be wondering, "Why is self-love so important?" It's a question worth asking, especially in a world that often encourages us to put others first or to strive relentlessly for external success. But consider this: self-love is the foundation of a fulfilled and balanced life. When you love and accept yourself, you can handle life's challenges better. You can also build healthier and more important relationships, and live a life of joy, purpose, and peace. Self-love isn't about being perfect or having everything figured out; it's about embracing who you are—flaws and all—and recognizing that you are enough just as you are.

Let's explore what self-love means. It's not about being selfish or arrogant, as some might mistakenly believe. Rather, it's about recognizing your inherent worth and treating yourself with the same kindness, compassion, and respect that you would offer to someone you deeply care about. It's about understanding that you deserve good things—not because of your accomplishments or how you compare to others, but simply because you are you.

I remember a time when I struggled with self-love. I would constantly compare myself to others, always feeling like I fell short in some way. Whether it was at work, in social settings, or even scrolling through social media, I couldn't help but focus on what I lacked rather than what made me unique. This habit of comparison left me feeling inadequate, unhappy, and disconnected from my true self.

The turning point came when I decided to shift my focus. Instead of dwelling on what I didn't have, I began to appreciate what I did have—my strengths, my achievements, and the journey that had shaped me. It wasn't easy at first, but as I gradually learned to celebrate my unique qualities and let go of the need for external validation, I began to feel a profound sense of inner peace and happiness.

Practical Tips for Discovering Your Inner Beauty

1.Practice Gratitude Daily: Start each day by acknowledging at least three things you're grateful for about yourself. It could be a skill you've developed, a personality trait you admire, or even a small accomplishment from the day before. This simple practice can shift your focus from what you lack to what you already have.

2.Create a Self-Love Journal: Dedicate a notebook to your journey of self-love. Write down your thoughts, feelings, and reflections as you navigate this path. Include positive affirmations, quotes that inspire you, and notes of encouragement to yourself. Over time, this journal will become a powerful tool for self-reflection and growth.

3.Surround Yourself with Positivity: The people you spend time with, the content you consume, and the environment you live in all influence how you feel about yourself. Surround yourself with people who uplift and support you, consume media that inspires you, and create a living space that feels like a sanctuary.

4.Focus on Your Strengths: Take time to identify your unique strengths and talents. What are you good at? What do people often compliment you on? Write these down and remind yourself of them regularly. When you focus on your strengths, you build confidence and resilience.

5.Practice Self-Compassion: When you make a mistake or face a setback, treat yourself with kindness rather than harsh criticism. Remember that everyone makes mistakes, and these experiences are growth opportunities. Speak to yourself as you would to a dear friend in a similar situation.

6.Meditate or Practice Mindfulness: Spend a few minutes each day in quiet reflection or mindfulness meditation. This practice can help you connect with your inner self, reduce stress, and cultivate a deeper sense of self-awareness and acceptance.

7.Affirmations: Start using positive affirmations daily. Statements like "I am worthy," "I am enough," and "I love and accept myself as I am" can help reprogram your mind to think positively about yourself.

8.Set Boundaries: Learn to say no to things that drain your energy or make you feel less than your best. Protect your time and energy, and prioritize activities that nourish your soul.

By incorporating these practices into your daily routine, you'll begin to see a shift in how you view yourself. You'll start to uncover the beauty that lies within and build a foundation of self-love that will support you throughout your life.

*****

CHAPTER TWO

Letting Go of Perfection

"Now that we've begun the journey of discovering the beauty within, let's address one of the biggest barriers to self-love: the pursuit of perfection. Let's get one thing straight: there's no such thing as perfect. Yet, many of us spend so much energy trying to reach this impossible goal. I've been there, and let me tell you, it's exhausting.
"

We live in a world that often glorifies perfection. Whether it's the flawless images we see on social media, the pressure to excel in every aspect of life, or the constant comparison to others, the message is clear: perfection is the goal. But here's the truth: perfection is an illusion. No one is perfect, and striving for perfection only leads to frustration, stress, and a sense of never being good enough.

I'd like to share a story about my friend. Anvi used to be a perfectionist. She would spend hours redoing tasks, trying to make everything flawless. She was meticulous about her work, her appearance, and even how she presented herself to others. But instead of feeling satisfied, she was often stressed, anxious, and unhappy. The constant pressure to be perfect was taking a toll on her mental and physical health.

It wasn't until Anvi had a heart-to-heart with herself that she realized something important: perfection is a myth. She began to understand that her worth wasn't tied to how perfectly she performed or how flawlessly she appeared. started embracing her mistakes and imperfections as part of her journey. She allowed herself to be human, to make mistakes, and to learn from them. And guess what? She felt a weight lift off her shoulders. She became happier, more productive, and more at ease with herself.

The lesson here is simple: Don't strive for perfection. Strive for progress. Celebrate your small wins, learn from your mistakes, and remember that it's okay to be a work-in-progress. Life is about growth, not about reaching some unattainable standard of perfection.

Practical Tips for Letting Go of Perfection

1. **Set Realistic Goals:** Instead of aiming for perfection, set realistic and achievable goals. Break down big tasks into smaller, manageable steps. This will help you focus on progress rather than perfection.

1. **Embrace Mistakes as Learning Opportunities:** When you make a mistake, don't beat yourself up. Instead, ask yourself, "What can I learn from this?" View mistakes

as opportunities for growth and improvement, not as failures.

3. **Practice Self-Compassion:** Perfectionism often stems from a fear of not being good enough. Combat this by practicing self-compassion. Remind yourself that it's okay to be imperfect and that you're doing your best.

4. **Limit Social Media:** Social media can be a breeding ground for comparison and perfectionism. Limit your time on social media and unfollow accounts that make you feel inadequate. Focus on the following accounts that inspire and uplift you.

5. **Celebrate Progress:** Take time to celebrate your progress, no matter how small. Recognize the effort you're putting in and the steps you're taking toward your goals. Celebrating progress will help you stay motivated and positive.

6. **Let Go of Control:** Accept that you can't control everything, and that's okay. Sometimes, things won't go as planned, and that's a part of life. Learn to go with the flow and adapt to changes without stressing over perfection.

7. **Surround Yourself with Supportive People:** Surround yourself with people who support and encourage you, rather than those who expect perfection. Having a strong support system can help you stay grounded and focused on what really matters.

8. **Practice Mindfulness:** Mindfulness can help you stay present and focused on the moment, rather than worrying about being perfect. Practice mindfulness techniques like deep breathing, meditation, or simply paying attention to your surroundings.

9. **Adopt a Growth Mindset:** Instead of seeing challenges as threats to your self-worth, view them as opportunities to grow and improve. A growth mindset encourages you to see potential rather than flaws.

By letting go of perfection, you free yourself from the constant pressure and stress that can drain your energy and happiness. You allow yourself to be human, to grow, and to enjoy the journey rather than obsessing over the destination. Remember, it's not about being perfect; it's about being authentic, real, and true to yourself.

As you continue on this journey of self-love, keep these lessons close to your heart. Embrace yourself, flaws and all, and remember that you are enough just as you are.

*****

CHAPTER THREE

Accepting Your Flaws

"We all have flaws. Whether they show up as being too critical of ourselves, fearing failure, or struggling with our self-image, these imperfections are part of what makes us human. It's easy to think that our flaws make us less worthy of love and respect, but the truth is, they do the opposite. Our flaws are what make us unique and relatable, and learning to accept them is a vital step in the journey toward self-love."

I used to be my own worst critic. Whenever I made a mistake, I'd beat myself up for days, replaying the situation over and over in my mind. I'd ask myself why I wasn't good enough, why I couldn't get things right. This cycle of self-criticism became a heavy burden, and it chipped away at my confidence and happiness.

But something changed when I decided to look at my flaws differently. I realized that my imperfections didn't define me. Instead, they were opportunities for growth, learning, and self-improvement. This shift in perspective allowed me to be kinder to myself, and as a result, I became more confident and happier.

<u>Understanding and Acknowledging Your Flaws</u>

The first step in accepting your flaws is understanding and acknowledging them without judgment. This may sound simple, but it can be one of the most challenging parts of the journey. We live in a society that often encourages perfection and hides imperfections. As a result, we tend to push our flaws into the background, hoping they'll disappear if we don't acknowledge them. But avoiding our flaws doesn't make them go away; it only gives them more power over us.

Take some time to reflect on the areas of your life where you feel less than perfect. Do you often criticize yourself for not meeting your own or others' expectations? Do you fear failure to the point where it prevents you from taking risks? Are you unhappy with aspects of your physical appearance or personality? Write these thoughts down in a journal or simply say them out loud to yourself. The key is to acknowledge these feelings without attaching negative emotions or judgments to them.

Remember, nobody is perfect. Every person you admire has their own set of flaws and insecurities, even if they don't show it. Accepting your flaws means recognizing that they are a natural part of being human. It doesn't mean you have to love every aspect of yourself immediately, but it does mean you're willing to embrace all parts of who you are.

<u>Transforming Flaws into Strengths</u>

Once you've acknowledged your flaws, the next step is to consider how you can transform them into strengths or learning opportunities. This process involves a shift in mindset—from seeing your flaws as weaknesses to viewing them as chances for personal growth.

For example, if you're someone who tends to be overly critical of yourself, try to reframe this trait as a strength. Your ability to notice details and strive for excellence can be valuable in many areas of life. However, it's important to balance this by being kind and forgiving toward yourself when things don't go perfectly. Recognize that it's okay to make mistakes, and that these mistakes are often where the most growth occurs.

If you struggle with a fear of failure, consider how this fear has held you back. Instead of letting it paralyze, you, use it as motivation to take calculated risks. Remind yourself that failure is not the end but a stepping stone to success. Many of the most successful people in the world have experienced significant failures before achieving their goals. By facing your fear of failure, you open yourself up to new possibilities and opportunities for growth.

If your self-image is something you wrestle with, try to focus on the things you like about yourself rather than fixating on what you wish were different. Celebrate your unique features, talents, and qualities. Remember, beauty isn't just about appearance; it's about how you feel about yourself and how you treat others.

Practical Tips for Accepting Your Flaws

1. **Practice Self-Compassion:** When you notice yourself being critical, pause and ask, "Would I say this to a friend?" If the answer is no, it's time to practice self-compassion. Speak to yourself with kindness and understanding, especially when you're struggling.

1. **Use Positive Affirmations:** Affirmations are a powerful tool to help reprogram your mind to think more positively about yourself. Start your day with affirmations like, "I accept myself as I am," "My flaws make me unique," or "I am worthy of love and respect."

3. **Seek Perspective from Others:** Sometimes we were our own worst critics. Talk to someone you trust about your perceived flaws. You might be surprised to find that what you see as a flaw, they see as a strength or don't notice at all.

4. **Focus on Your Accomplishments:** When you feel down about your flaws, take a moment to reflect on your accomplishments. Remind yourself of the things you've achieved and the challenges you've overcome. This can help you see yourself in a more balanced light.

5. **Limit Comparison:** Comparing yourself to others is a sure way to amplify your flaws and diminish your strengths. Remember that everyone's journey is different, and what you perceive as a flaw may be a source of pride for someone else. Focus on your own path and progress.

6. **Embrace Imperfection:** Start small by allowing yourself to be imperfect in certain areas of your life. For example, if you're a perfectionist at your work, give yourself permission to make small mistakes without overanalyzing them. This practice can help you become more comfortable with your flaws.

7. **Surround Yourself with Positivity:** Spend time with people who uplift and encourage you. Being around positive influences can help you feel more confident and less focused on your flaws. Additionally, engage with content that promotes self-acceptance and positivity.

8. **Meditate on Self-Acceptance:** Meditation can be a powerful tool for cultivating self-acceptance. Spend a few minutes each day focusing on your breath and repeating a mantra like, "I accept myself fully, flaws and all." This practice can help you internalize self-acceptance over time.

9. **Focus on Personal Growth:** Instead of viewing your flaws as static, see them as opportunities for growth. Set personal development goals that align with your values and work on them gradually. By focusing on growth, you'll see your flaws as part of a larger journey of self-improvement.

10.**Celebrate Your Uniqueness:** Recognize that your flaws are part of what makes you unique. They contribute to your story and your character. Embrace your quirks and imperfections as integral parts of who you are.

The Power of Self-Acceptance

As you work on accepting your flaws, you'll notice a shift in how you perceive yourself and how you interact with the world around you. Self-acceptance leads to greater self-confidence, resilience, and inner peace. When you stop fighting against your flaws and start embracing them, you free up energy to focus on what truly matters—living a fulfilling, authentic life.

Remember, accepting your flaws doesn't mean you have to love every aspect of yourself right away. It's a process that takes time, patience, and practice. But with each step you take, you'll move closer to a deeper sense of self-love and acceptance.

In the end, your flaws are not roadblocks; they're stepping stones on your journey to becoming the best version of yourself. Embrace them, learn from them, and allow them to guide you toward a more authentic, empowered life.

*****

Positive Changes, One Step at a Time

"Change can be intimidating, especially when you feel like there's a mountain of things you need to improve on. But here's the thing: change doesn't have to happen all at once. In fact, the most lasting and meaningful changes often occur gradually, one small step at a time. This approach makes change feel more manageable and less overwhelming, allowing you to build momentum and confidence as you progress."

Take my cousin Aditya, for example. For years, Aditya struggled with his health. He was overweight, tired, and generally unhappy with how he felt every day. He knew he needed to make changes, but the idea of completely overhauling his lifestyle seemed impossible. The thought of strict diets, intense workout regimens, and giving up his favorite foods all at once was too much to handle. So, Aditya did something different—he started small.

Aditya didn't sign up for a gym membership or toss out all the junk food in his house overnight. Instead, he began by adding a short walk to his daily routine. It wasn't much, just a 15-minute stroll around the block, but it was something he could commit to. As the weeks passed, Aditya found that he enjoyed these walks. They gave him time to clear his mind and get some fresh air. Once walking became a habit, he felt more motivated to make other small changes.

He began incorporating more fruits and vegetables into his meals, not by cutting out all his favorite foods, but by adding healthier options alongside them. He started drinking more water, replacing just one soda a day with a glass of water. These changes were so gradual that they didn't feel like a chore or a punishment. Over time, Aditya's small efforts started to add up. He lost weight, gained energy, and most importantly, felt better about himself.

This story illustrates a powerful truth: you don't need to make huge changes all at once. Start with something small, something that feels doable, and build on it. Before you know it, those small changes will lead to big results.

Practical Tips for Making Positive Changes

1.**Set Small, Achievable Goals:** Instead of aiming for a massive transformation, break your goal down into smaller, more manageable steps. For example, if you want to get healthier, start by adding a 10-minute walk to your daily routine rather than committing to an hour-long workout every day.

2.**Focus on One Change at a Time:** Trying to change too many things at once can be overwhelming and lead to burnout. Choose one area of your life to focus on and give it your full attention. Once you've made progress in that area, move on to the next.

3.Celebrate Small Wins: Every step forward is progress, no matter how small. Celebrate your achievements, whether it's sticking to a new habit for a week or making a healthier choice at lunch. Recognizing your progress will keep you motivated.

4.Be Patient with Yourself: Change takes time. There will be setbacks, and that's okay. What matters is that you keep going, even when things don't go perfectly. Be kind to yourself and remember that every step forward is a step in the right direction.

5.Create a Support System: Share your goals with friends or family members who can encourage and support you. Having someone to cheer you on or hold you accountable can make a big difference in staying on track.

6.Track Your Progress: Keep a journal or use an app to track your progress. Seeing your improvements over time can boost your confidence and keep you motivated to continue.

7.Reward Yourself: When you reach a milestone, treat yourself to something special. It doesn't have to be extravagant—maybe it's a movie night, a new book, or a small indulgence. Rewards can reinforce your positive behavior and make the process more enjoyable.

8.Stay Flexible: Life is unpredictable, and sometimes things won't go as planned. Be flexible and willing to adjust your goals or approach as needed. What's important is that you keep moving forward, even if it's in a slightly different direction than you initially planned.

9.Visualize Your Success: Take a few moments each day to visualize yourself achieving your goal. Imagine how you'll feel, what your life will look like, and the benefits you'll enjoy. Visualization can help keep you focused and motivated.

10. Keep the Big Picture in Mind: While it's important to focus on small steps, don't lose sight of your goal. Remind yourself why you're making these changes and the positive impact they'll have on your life.

The Ripple Effect of Positive Change

One of the most powerful aspects of making small, positive changes is the ripple effect they can have on other areas of your life. When you start to see progress in one area, it often motivates you to make changes in other areas as well. For example, once Aditya started feeling healthier from his daily walks and improved diet, he found that he had more energy and confidence to tackle other goals, like improving his relationships and advancing his career.

Positive changes build on each other. The more you accomplish, the more you believe in your ability to make even bigger changes. This creates a cycle of growth and self-improvement that can transform your life over time.

Real-Life Success Stories

Let's look at a few more examples of how small changes can lead to big results:

- **Anam's Financial Journey:** Anam was overwhelmed by her debt and didn't know where to start. Instead of trying to pay off everything at once, she focused on paying an extra Rs.5000 a month toward her smallest debt. As she saw her balance decrease, she felt motivated to increase her payments. Over time, she paid off that debt and moved on to the next. Today, Anam is debt-free, all because she started with one small step.

- **Divyendra's Career Growth:** Divendra wanted to advance in his career but felt stuck in his current position. He decided to start by taking an online course in his field. This small step led to new skills, which boosted his confidence. He then took on additional responsibilities at work and eventually earned a promotion.

- **Saumya's Journey to Self-Love:** Saumya struggled with low self-esteem for years. She decided to start by practicing positive affirmations each morning. This small change helped her shift her mindset, and over time, she began to feel more confident. This newfound self-love motivated her to pursue her passions, leading to a more fulfilling life.

These stories highlight the power of taking small, consistent steps toward positive change. No matter how big or small your goal is, remember that every step counts and that progress is possible.

Embracing the Journey

As you work on making positive changes in your life, remember that it's a journey, not a destination. There will be times when progress feels slow, and there will be setbacks along the way. But each step you take, no matter how small, brings you closer to the life you want to live.

Change can be challenging, but it's also incredibly rewarding. By taking it one step at a time, you give yourself the best chance of success. So, start small, stay committed, and watch as those small steps lead to big, positive changes in your life.

*****

CHAPTER FIVE

Practicing Gratitude

"Gratitude is one of the most transformative practices you can adopt on your journey to self-love. It's simple, accessible, and doesn't require any special tools or resources—just a willingness to shift your focus. When you actively practice gratitude, you begin to see life through a different lens. Instead of constantly dwelling on what you lack or what's wrong, you start to notice and appreciate the abundance and goodness that already exist in your life."

The Power of Gratitude

Gratitude is more than just saying "thank you" or feeling happy when things go your way. It's a deep sense of appreciation for the small and big blessings that life offers you daily. When you focus on gratitude, you're essentially telling yourself that you recognize and value what you have, which in turn reinforces a positive mindset.

Research has shown that practicing gratitude can lead to numerous mental and physical health benefits. These include reduced stress, improved mood, better sleep, and even a stronger immune system. Gratitude helps shift your focus away from negative emotions like envy, resentment, and frustration and instead fosters feelings of contentment, happiness, and peace.

My Journey with Gratitude

For many years, I struggled with feeling inadequate. I often focused on what was missing in my life—whether it was material possessions, achievements, or personal qualities I thought I lacked. This mindset left me feeling dissatisfied and unhappy, no matter how much I accomplished or acquired.

It wasn't until a friend introduced me to the practice of gratitude that things began to change. They suggested I start a gratitude journal, where I would write down three things I was grateful for each night before bed. At first, it felt a bit forced, and I struggled to come up with things to be grateful for. But as I continued the practice, something remarkable happened. I noticed the small, positive details in my day that I had previously overlooked.

Instead of dwelling on the negative, I started appreciating the warmth of the sun on my face, the laughter shared with a friend or the delicious meal I enjoyed. These were simple moments, but acknowledging them brought a profound sense of joy and contentment into my life. Over time, I noticed a shift in my overall mindset. I became more optimistic, more resilient in the face of challenges, and more at peace with myself.

Practical Tips for Cultivating Gratitude

<u>**Now that you understand the power of gratitude, let's explore some practical ways to incorporate it into your daily life.**</u>

1. **Start a Gratitude Journal:** This is one of the most effective ways to practice gratitude. Each night, take a few minutes to write down three to five things you're grateful for. They can be as small as enjoying a cup of coffee in the morning or as significant as a promotion at work. The key is consistency—by making this a daily habit, you train your mind to focus on the positive aspects of your life.

1. **Express Gratitude to Others:** Don't keep your gratitude to yourself—share it with those around you. Take time to thank the people who make your life better, whether it's a family member, a friend, a colleague, or even a stranger who showed you kindness. Expressing gratitude not only strengthens your relationships but also deepens your own sense of appreciation.

3. **Practice Mindful Gratitude:** Throughout your day, pause and take a moment to appreciate the present moment. This could be while you're eating a meal, enjoying nature, or simply sitting quietly. Focus on what you're experiencing and acknowledge how fortunate you are to have that moment.

4. **Create a Gratitude Ritual:** Integrate gratitude into your daily routine by creating a ritual around it. For example, you might start each day by thinking of one thing you're grateful for before getting out of bed. Or, you could end your day by reflecting on something positive that

happened. These rituals help reinforce a habit of gratitude.

5. **Gratitude Walks:** Take a walk outside and use this time to focus on what you're grateful for. As you walk, pay attention to your surroundings—the beauty of nature, the sounds, the fresh air—and let these observations fill you with a sense of gratitude.

6. **Turn Challenges into Opportunities for Gratitude:** It's easy to be thankful when things are going well, but the real challenge is finding gratitude in hard situations. When you face challenges, try to find something good that could happen from it. This could be a lesson-learned, personal growth, or an opportunity to improve your strength.

7. **Gratitude Jar:** Put a jar in a place where people can see it. When something good happens, write it down on paper and put it in the jar. At the end of the year, or whenever you need a reminder, open the jar and read through all the things you were grateful for. It's a powerful way to see just how much good has come into your life.

8. **Morning Gratitude Meditation:** Start your day with a short gratitude meditation. Sit quietly and focus on your breathing. Then, think of three things you're grateful for and hold that feeling of gratitude in your heart as you begin your day. This sets a positive tone for the rest of your day.

9. **Gratitude Affirmations:** Make a list of gratitude affirmations that you feel good about. For example, you could say, "I am thankful for the love and support in my life" or, "I am thankful for the abundance around me." Repeat these affirmations daily to reinforce a mindset of gratitude.

10.**Gratitude Letters:** Write a letter to someone who has made a positive impact on your life. Express your gratitude for their kindness, support, or influence. You don't have to send the letter if you don't want to—the act of writing it is powerful.

The Ripple Effect of Gratitude

One of the most beautiful aspects of practicing gratitude is how it can create a ripple effect in your life. When you focus on the positive and appreciate what you have, you're more likely to attract more positivity and abundance. This doesn't mean that life will always be perfect or free of challenges, but gratitude helps you navigate those challenges with a more resilient and optimistic mindset.

Moreover, when you practice gratitude, you become more mindful and present in your daily life. You start to notice and savor the small moments that bring you joy, rather than constantly chasing after the next big thing. This change in thinking can make you happier and more fulfilled. You will realize that happiness is not something you can get in the future. It is something you can have now.

Gratitude also strengthens your relationships. When you express appreciation to others, you build deeper connections and foster a sense of belonging. People naturally gravitate toward those who acknowledge and value them, and as a result, your relationships become more positive and supportive.

Real-Life Stories of Gratitude

Let me share a few stories that highlight the impact of gratitude:

- ◦ **Sikha's Story:** Shikha was going through a difficult time after losing her job. She felt overwhelmed by fear and uncertainty about the future. A friend suggested she start a gratitude journal. At first, Sikha found it hard to find things to be grateful for, but she persisted. She began to appreciate the support of her family, the extra time she had to pursue hobbies, and the small acts of kindness from friends. Over time, this practice helped Maria shift her focus from fear to possibility, and she eventually found a new job that she loved.

- ◦ **Utkarsh's Story:** Utkarsh was dealing with chronic pain that affected his daily life. Instead of focusing on what he couldn't do, he decided to practice gratitude for the things he could still enjoy, like spending time with loved ones, listening to music, and reading. This shift in perspective didn't take away his pain, but it made it more bearable and allowed him to find joy in his struggles.

- ◦ **Ankita's Story:** Ankita was constantly stressed about her busy schedule and felt like she was always rushing from one task to the next. She decided to incorporate gratitude into her daily routine by taking a few minutes each morning to reflect on what she was thankful for.

This simple practice helped her start her day with a positive mindset, and she found that she was better able to handle the demands of her busy life.

These stories demonstrate that gratitude isn't just a feel-good practice—it's a powerful tool for transforming your life, even in the face of challenges.

Embracing Gratitude as a Lifelong Practice

As you begin your own gratitude journey, remember that it's not about being perfect or forcing yourself to feel grateful when you don't. Gratitude is a practice, and like any practice, it takes time and patience to cultivate. Some days it will come easily, and other days it might be more challenging. The key is to stay consistent and to be gentle with yourself as you develop this habit.

Gratitude is a lifelong practice that can bring immense joy, peace, and fulfillment into your life. By regularly focusing on what you're grateful for, you open yourself up to experiencing life in a richer, more meaningful way. So, start today—take a few moments to reflect on the good in your life, and watch as this simple practice begins to transform your outlook and your world.

*****

CHAPTER SIX

Surrounding Yourself with Positivity

"The people we surround ourselves with play a crucial role in shaping our self-esteem, happiness, and overall outlook on life. The energy and attitudes of those in our inner circle can either uplift us or pull us down, impacting our mental and emotional well-being. If you're constantly around negativity, it's almost impossible to maintain a positive outlook. This chapter will explore the importance of surrounding yourself with positivity and provide practical tips on how to cultivate a supportive and encouraging environment."

The Impact of Your Social Circle

We often underestimate the influence our social circle has on us. The people you spend the most time with can shape your thoughts, behaviors, and even your beliefs about yourself. If you're surrounded by individuals who are negative, critical, or unsupportive, their attitudes will seep into your own mindset, making it difficult for you to stay positive and confident.

On the other hand, when you surround yourself with positive, encouraging people, you're more likely to adopt a similar outlook on life. Positive energy is contagious. When you have people who are happy, supportive, and kind, it's easier to stay positive and feel good about yourself.

My Experience with Negativity

I once had a friend who was constantly negative. No matter what good news I shared or how excited I was about something, they would always find a way to bring me down. If I got a promotion at work, they'd say something like, "Well, don't get too comfortable—they might cut jobs next year." If I mentioned going on a vacation, they'd remind me of all the potential things that could go wrong. Over time, I noticed that being around them was draining my energy and making me feel bad about myself. I started doubting my own achievements and feeling anxious about things that I should have been celebrating.

It took me a while to realize that this friend's negativity was having such a profound impact on me. But once I did, I knew I had to make a change. I made the difficult decision to distance myself from her and began spending more time with people who uplifted and supported me. The difference was incredible. I felt lighter, happier, and more confident. My outlook on life became more optimistic, and I found it easier to maintain a positive mindset.

Practical Tips for Cultivating a Positive Social Circle

Now that you understand the importance of surrounding yourself with positivity, let's dive into some practical steps you can take to create a supportive and encouraging environment.

1. Evaluate Your Current Relationships

Take a close look at the people in your life. Are they lifting you up or dragging you down? Make a list of your closest friends, family members, and colleagues, and consider how each person makes you feel. Do they encourage and support you, or do they often criticize and bring negativity into your life? It's important to be honest with yourself during this process.

2. Set Boundaries with Negative Influences

If you identify people in your life who consistently bring negativity, it's time to set some boundaries. This doesn't necessarily mean cutting them out of your life completely (unless the relationship is toxic), but it does mean limiting the amount of time and energy you spend on these interactions. For example, if a coworker always complains and makes you feel bad, try to avoid talking to them or talk about more positive things.

3. Seek Out Positive, Like-Minded Individuals

Actively seek out relationships with people who share your values, goals, and outlook on life. Join clubs, groups, or communities that align with your interests, whether it's a hobby, a fitness group, or a volunteer organization. Surrounding yourself with like-minded individuals who are positive and supportive will naturally elevate your own mood and mindset.

4. Nurture Relationships with Positive People

Once you've identified the positive influences in your life, try to nurture those relationships. Spend more time with people who make you feel good about yourself and who encourage you to grow. These are friends who celebrate your successes, listen to your concerns without judgment, and provide support when you need it. Invest time and energy into these relationships, and let these people know how much you appreciate their positivity and support.

5.Be the Positivity You Want to See

Remember that positivity is a two-way street. If you want to be surrounded by positive people, you also need to be a source of positivity yourself. Practice kindness, encouragement, and optimism in your interactions with others. When you radiate positive energy, you'll naturally attract others who do the same. This doesn't mean you have to always be happy, but trying to be positive will help create a supportive environment.

6. Limit Exposure to Negative Media

In addition to evaluating the people in your life, consider the media you consume. Constant exposure to negative news, toxic social media, and other forms of media that promote fear or pessimism can have a detrimental effect on your mindset. Try to balance your media consumption with positive, uplifting content that inspires and motivates you. Follow social media accounts that promote positivity, read books that encourage personal growth, and watch movies or shows that make you feel good.

7. Create a Positive Physical Environment

Your physical surroundings can also have a significant impact on your mood and mindset. Create a space in your home or office that is conducive to positivity. This could involve decluttering, adding plants, incorporating uplifting artwork, or simply ensuring that your environment is clean and organized. A positive physical environment can help reinforce a positive mental environment.

8. Practice Gratitude in Your Relationships

Gratitude is a powerful tool for enhancing positivity in your relationships. Make it a habit to express gratitude to the people in your life who bring positivity and support. Whether it's a sincere thank you, a kind note, or just saying how much they helped you, saying Thanks makes your connections stronger and encourages more good interactions.

9. Distance Yourself from Toxic Relationships

Sometimes, despite our best efforts, certain relationships remain toxic and detrimental to our well-being. In such cases, it may be necessary to distance yourself or even end the relationship altogether. This can be very hard, especially if the person is a close friend or family member. But your mental and emotional health should always be the most important thing. Trust that by letting go of toxic relationships, you're making space for more positive, supportive people to enter your life.

10. Surround Yourself with Inspirational Content

In addition to positive people, surround yourself with content that inspires and uplifts you. This could be in the form of books, podcasts, videos, or even quotes that resonate with you. Create a vision board with images and affirmations that reflect the life you want to live and the person you want to be. Having these positive reminders in your daily environment can help keep you focused on your goals and maintain a positive mindset.

The Ripple Effect of Positivity

When you surround yourself with positivity, the effects ripple out into every aspect of your life. A positive environment boosts your self-esteem, enhances your resilience in the face of challenges, and helps you maintain a healthy outlook on life. It also strengthens your relationships, as positivity fosters deeper connections and mutual support.

Moreover, as you cultivate a positive environment, you become a source of positivity for others. Your energy, attitude, and actions can inspire those around you to adopt a more positive mindset. This ripple effect not only improves your own life but also contributes to a more positive and uplifting community.

Real-Life Examples of the Power of Positivity

Let me share a few stories that illustrate the impact of surrounding yourself with positivity:

- **Vartika's Story**: Vartika was feeling stuck in a job she didn't enjoy and was surrounded by colleagues who constantly complained about their work. She noticed that their negativity was affecting her own attitude and motivation. Vartika decided to make a change. She joined a professional networking group that focused on personal development and positive thinking. Through this group, she met new friends who encouraged and supported her. Inspired by their positivity, Vartika eventually found the courage to pursue a career change, leading to a more fulfilling and happy life.

- **Deepak's Story**: Deepak had always been close to his family, but he realized that certain family members were consistently negative and critical. Their comments often left him feeling inadequate and discouraged. After much reflection, Deepak decided to set boundaries and limit his interactions with these family members. He began spending more time with friends who were supportive and uplifting. As a result, Deepak's confidence grew, and he felt more empowered to pursue his passions and goals.

- **Alia's Story:** Alia was having a hard time after a breakup. Her friends were more interested in gossip and drama than in helping her. She realized that these friendships were not contributing to her healing or personal growth. Alia made the tough decision to distance herself from these friends and instead joined a support group where she met others who were going through similar experiences. The positive energy and encouragement she received from the group helped her heal and regain her sense of self-worth.

These stories highlight the profound impact that surrounding yourself with positivity can have on your life. It's not always easy to change your social circle, but the benefits are well worth the effort.

Embracing Positivity as a Lifelong Practice

Creating and maintaining a positive environment is an ongoing process. It requires continuous effort, self-awareness, and sometimes difficult decisions. But as you commit to surrounding yourself with positivity, you'll find that your life becomes richer, more fulfilling, and more joyful.

Remember that positivity doesn't mean ignoring challenges or pretending everything is perfect. It's about choosing to focus on the good, seeking out supportive relationships, and cultivating an environment that nurtures your well-being. By surrounding yourself with positivity, you create a strong foundation for self-love, resilience, and happiness.

*****

CHAPTER SEVEN

The Power of Self-Care

"Self-care is often misunderstood as merely indulging in occasional pampering. However, it encompasses much more than that. It's a fundamental practice that involves taking deliberate actions to nurture your mind, body, and soul. It's about understanding your needs, setting boundaries, and ensuring that you are prioritizing your well-being. In this chapter, we'll explore the true essence of self-care, share personal experiences, and offer practical tips to help you integrate self-care into your daily life."

Understanding the True Meaning of Self-Care

Self-care is more than just treating yourself to a spa day or buying a new gadget. It's about creating a balanced life by addressing and fulfilling your emotional, physical, and mental needs. It involves recognizing when you're feeling overwhelmed, stressed, or depleted and taking proactive steps to restore your energy and well-being.

A few years ago, I found myself caught in a cycle of overwork and constant busyness. My calendar was filled with commitments, and I rarely took time for myself. I was saying yes to every request, driven by a desire to be helpful and reliable. However, this approach left me exhausted and burnt out. My health suffered, and my productivity declined. It was then I realized that I couldn't continue pouring from an empty cup. I needed to prioritize self-care.

<u>Practical Tips for Effective Self-Care</u>

1. Set Boundaries and Learn to Say No

One of the most significant aspects of self-care is setting boundaries. This means knowing your limits and being willing to say no when necessary. Many of us struggle with this because we fear disappointing others or missing out. However, over-committing ourselves can lead to burnout and decreased quality of work.

Tip: Practice saying no in a kind but firm manner. For example, you might say, "I appreciate you thinking of me, but I'm unable to take on this task right now. Perhaps someone else could assist you." Remember, setting boundaries is about protecting your well-being, not about being selfish.

2. Prioritize Sleep

Sleep is crucial for overall health and well-being. Lack of adequate rest can affect your mood, cognitive function, and physical health. It's essential to establish a consistent sleep schedule and create a restful environment.

Tip: Develop a bedtime routine that promotes relaxation. This could include activities such as reading a book, practicing deep breathing exercises, or taking a warm bath. Avoid screens and stimulating activities at least an hour before bed to help your body wind down.

3. Adopt a Balanced Diet

Nutrition plays a vital role in how we feel physically and emotionally. Eating a balanced diet with plenty of fruits, vegetables, lean proteins, and whole grains can boost your energy levels and overall mood.

Tip: Plan your meals ahead of time to ensure you're making healthy choices. Keep nutritious snacks, like nuts or fruit, handy for when you're on the go. Hydrate well by drinking plenty of water throughout the day.

4. Incorporate Regular Exercise

Physical activity is not only beneficial for your body but also for your mind. Exercise can reduce stress, improve mood, and enhance overall health. You don't need to engage in intense workouts; even moderate activities like walking or yoga can be highly effective.

Tip: Find an exercise routine that you enjoy and can stick with. This could be a daily walk, a dance class, or a home workout video. Make it a part of your routine and set achievable goals to stay motivated.

5. Engage in Activities That Bring Joy

Self-care involves doing things that make you happy and fulfilled. Whether it's a hobby, spending time with loved ones, or simply relaxing, it's important to allocate time for activities that bring you joy.

Tip: Make a list of activities that you enjoy and schedule them into your week. This could be anything from painting, gardening, or playing a musical instrument. Regularly engaging in these activities helps to recharge your emotional batteries.

6. Practice Mindfulness and Relaxation Techniques

Mindfulness and relaxation techniques, such as meditation and deep breathing exercises, can help reduce stress and promote mental clarity. These practices allow you to stay present and manage your thoughts and emotions more effectively.

Tip: Start with a few minutes of mindfulness practice each day. You can use apps or guided meditation videos to help you get started. Set aside a quiet space where you can practice without interruptions.

7. Seek Professional Help When Needed

Sometimes, self-care involves recognizing when you need additional support. If you're struggling with mental health issues, such as anxiety or depression, seeking help from a mental health professional is a crucial step in taking care of yourself.

Tip: Don't hesitate to reach out for professional support if you need it. Therapists, counselors, and support groups can provide valuable tools and strategies to help you manage your mental health and well-being.

8. Cultivate Positive Relationships

Surrounding yourself with supportive and uplifting individuals is an important aspect of self-care. Positive relationships can provide encouragement, understanding, and a sense of belonging.

Tip: Evaluate your current relationships and focus on nurturing those that bring positivity into your life. Spend quality time with friends and family who support and uplift you. Try to connect with people who share your values and interests.

9. Create a Self-Care Routine

Establishing a self-care routine ensures that you're consistently taking time to address your needs. This routine should include activities and practices that support your overall well-being.

Tip: Develop a self-care plan that outlines daily, weekly, and monthly practices. For example, daily self-care could include journaling or a morning stretch, while weekly self-care might involve a longer activity like a hike or a day trip. Regularly review and adjust your routine as needed.

10. Celebrate Your Progress

Self-care is an ongoing process, and it's important to acknowledge and celebrate your efforts. Recognize the positive changes you've made and the progress you've achieved.

Tip: Keep a self-care journal where you record your activities, feelings, and any improvements you notice. Reflect on your entries regularly to see how far you've come and to stay motivated.

The Benefits of Embracing Self-Care

<u>Prioritizing self-care can lead to numerous benefits, including:</u>

- **Enhanced Physical Health:** Regular self-care practices contribute to better physical health by reducing stress, improving sleep, and promoting healthy habits.

- **Improved Mental Well-Being:** Engaging in self-care helps manage stress, anxiety, and depression, leading to a more balanced and positive mental state.

- **Increased Productivity and Focus:** Taking care of yourself enables you to be more productive and focused, as you're not operating from a place of exhaustion.

- **Stronger Relationships:** When you prioritize self-care, you're more likely to have the energy and emotional capacity to invest in meaningful relationships.

- **Greater Self-Awareness**: Self-care practices foster greater self-awareness, helping you understand your needs, desires, and boundaries more clearly.

Real-Life Examples of Self-Care Success

<u>Let's look at some real-life examples of how prioritizing self-care has made a positive impact:</u>

- **Nivedita's Journey to Well-Being**: Nivedita was overwhelmed by her responsibilities as a single mother and a full-time employee. She struggled with fatigue and stress. After recognizing the need for self-care, Nivedita began setting boundaries at work and dedicated time each week to activities she enjoyed, such as reading and gardening. She also sought support from a therapist to manage her stress. Over time, Nivedita felt more balanced, energetic, and happier in her daily life.
- **Abhinandan's Transformation**: Abhinandan was dealing with burnout from a demanding job and felt disconnected from his passions. He decided to implement a self-care routine that included regular exercise, healthy eating, and mindfulness practices. By making self-care a priority, Abhinandan noticed significant improvements in his mood and productivity. He also reconnected with hobbies he had neglected, which brought him joy and fulfillment

- **Vaishnavi's New Perspective**: Vaishnavi struggled with self-esteem issues and often neglected her own needs in favor of pleasing others. After attending a self-care workshop, she learned the importance of setting boundaries and taking time for herself. Vaishnavi began practicing gratitude, engaging in hobbies, and spending quality time with supportive friends. These changes led to a boost in her self-confidence and overall well-being.

Embracing Self-Care as a Lifelong Practice

Self-care is not a one-time fix but a lifelong practice. It requires regular attention and adjustment to suit your evolving needs and circumstances. Embrace self-care as a continuous journey of nurturing yourself and prioritizing your well-being. By doing so, you'll create a strong foundation for a fulfilling and balanced life.

So take a moment to reflect on your current self-care practices. Are you adequately taking care of your mind, body, and soul? If not, consider implementing some of the practical tips mentioned above and make self-care a non-negotiable part of your routine. Remember, you deserve to prioritize your well-being and to live a life that feels fulfilling and joyful.

*****

CHAPTER EIGHT

Embracing Your Journey

"Self-love isn't a destination you reach; it's a journey you navigate. It's a continual process of growth, acceptance, and transformation. Embracing your journey means understanding that self-love involves both triumphs and challenges. It's about learning to appreciate and accept yourself through all the highs and lows. In this chapter, we'll delve into what it means to embrace your journey, share personal anecdotes, and provide practical tips to help you stay on course."

Understanding the Journey of Self-Love

Self-love is often portrayed as an ideal state of being, where one is perpetually confident and content. However, the reality is more nuanced. Self-love involves navigating a path filled with various experiences—some uplifting, others challenging. There will be moments when you feel on top of the world and others when you might question your worth or feel discouraged. The key is to understand that this ebb and flow is a natural part of your journey.

For me, embracing my journey has meant accepting that growth is not linear. There have been times when I've faced setbacks, made mistakes, and felt overwhelmed. Yet, each of these experiences has taught me valuable lessons and contributed to my personal development. It's essential to recognize that these moments of struggle are not failures but opportunities for learning and growth.

The Importance of Self-Acceptance

One of the most crucial aspects of embracing your journey is self-acceptance. It's about acknowledging and embracing who you are, including your strengths, weaknesses, and imperfections. Self-acceptance allows you to move forward with a sense of peace and authenticity.

There was a period in my life when I struggled with self-acceptance. I was constantly comparing myself to others and feeling inadequate. It wasn't until I began to appreciate my unique qualities and accept my imperfections that I started to feel more at ease with myself. This shift in mindset was transformative and allowed me to approach challenges with greater resilience.

Practical Tips for Embracing Your Journey

1. Reflect on Your Progress

Regularly take time to reflect on how far you've come. Acknowledge your achievements, no matter how small, and celebrate your progress. This practice helps to reinforce a positive mindset and reminds you of your growth.

Tip: Keep a journal where you record your milestones and reflections. Write about your successes, lessons learned from challenges, and moments of self-discovery. Review your journal periodically to see how much you've accomplished and how much you've grown.

2. Practice Self-Compassion

Be kind to yourself, especially during difficult times. Self-compassion involves treating yourself with the same kindness and understanding that you would offer a friend. It's about recognizing that everyone makes mistakes and that these are learning opportunities, not reasons for self-criticism.

Tip: When you face a setback or make a mistake, pause and offer yourself a kind affirmation. For example, you might say, "It's okay to make mistakes. I'm doing my best, and I will learn from this experience."

3. Set Realistic Goals

Setting achievable goals is an essential part of your journey. Goals give you direction and purpose but ensure they are realistic and aligned with your current circumstances. Setting yourself up for success involves creating goals that are specific, measurable, attainable, relevant, and time-bound (smart).

Tip: Break down larger goals into smaller, manageable steps. For example, if your goal is to improve your fitness, start with small, achievable targets like a 10-minute daily workout, and gradually increase the intensity as you progress.

4. Embrace Your Unique Path

Remember that everyone's journey is unique. Avoid comparing yourself to others and focus on your personal growth and development. Embrace the path that is right for you, and trust that it will lead you to where you need to be.

Tip: Create a vision board that represents your personal goals, values, and aspirations. Use it as a reminder of your unique path and to stay motivated and focused on your journey.

5. Learn from Challenges

Challenges are an inevitable part of life, but they offer valuable growth opportunities. Instead of viewing challenges as obstacles, see them as chances to learn and evolve. Reflect on what you can gain from these experiences and how they can contribute to your development.

Tip: When faced with a challenge, ask yourself questions like, "What can I learn from this situation?" And "How can I use this experience to grow?" Document your insights and incorporate them into your journey.

6. Surround Yourself with Supportive People

The people you choose to surround yourself with can significantly impact your journey. Seek out individuals who uplift and support you, and who encourage your growth and self-love. Positive relationships can provide valuable perspective and motivation.

Tip: Evaluate your social circle and identify those who contribute positively to your life. Spend more time with these individuals and seek out new connections that align with your values and aspirations.

7. Practice Gratitude

Cultivating a sense of gratitude can help you stay grounded and focused on the positives in your life. Gratitude shifts your perspective from what you lack to what you have, enhancing your overall sense of well-being.

Tip: Start a daily gratitude practice by writing down three things you're thankful for each day. This simple habit can help you appreciate the positives in your life and foster a more optimistic outlook.

8. Be Patient with Yourself

Self-love and personal growth are ongoing processes. It's important to be patient with yourself and recognize that change takes time. Avoid rushing or pressuring yourself to achieve certain milestones quickly.

Tip: Set realistic expectations for yourself and acknowledge that progress is a gradual process. Celebrate small wins along the way and be patient as you continue to work towards your goals.

9. Seek Guidance When Needed

Sometimes, navigating your journey may require additional support or guidance. Don't hesitate to seek help from mentors, coaches, or therapists who can offer valuable insights and support.

Tip: Identify areas where you might benefit from external guidance and explore options for professional or personal support. Whether it's a career coach, a therapist, or a mentor, seeking help can provide valuable perspective and assistance.

10. Celebrate Your Achievements

Taking time to celebrate your achievements, no matter how small is an important aspect of embracing your journey. Recognizing and celebrating your successes reinforces positive behavior and motivates you to continue pursuing your goals.

Tip: Establish a habit of celebrating your achievements. This could be through a small treat, a personal reward, or simply taking a moment to acknowledge your hard work and progress.

Embracing Your Journey as a Lifelong Practice

Embracing your journey is not a one-time event but a lifelong practice. It requires ongoing effort, self-awareness, and a willingness to grow and evolve. By staying committed to your journey and applying the practical tips outlined above, you can cultivate a deeper sense of self-love and fulfillment.

Remember, your journey is uniquely yours. Embrace it with all its complexities, challenges, and triumphs. Be patient and compassionate with yourself, and keep moving forward with a sense of curiosity and optimism. As you continue to nurture and embrace your journey, you'll find that your life becomes richer, more meaningful, and more fulfilling.

So, take a moment to reflect on your journey so far. Acknowledge your growth, appreciate the lessons learned, and commit to embracing the path ahead. Your journey is a testament to your resilience, strength, and capacity for self-love. Embrace it fully, and you'll discover a life of profound fulfillment and joy.

*****

About The Author

Love yourself first, and everything else falls into line.
You have to love yourself to get anything done in this
world.-Lucille Ball

Piyush Singh is an ardent supporter of *self-love and personal growth*, hailing from **Chapra, Bihar, India**. With a **Master's degree in Psychology**, Piyush has gained a deep understanding of the human mind and behavior and is dedicated to helping others cultivate a more compassionate and loving relationship with themselves.

Through his writing and work, Piyush aims to inspire individuals to break free from self-doubt and negativity and tap into their inner strength and potential. His approach is rooted in empathy, kindness, and a deep understanding of the human experience.

"Self Love Symphony" is Piyush's ***debut book***, born out of a desire to share the transformative power of self-love with a wider audience. He hopes that his words will inspire readers to embark on their journey of self-discovery and growth and live a life filled with purpose, joy, and love.

Afterword

As we reach the final notes of this symphony, I hope that the melodies of self-love have resonated deep within your heart. May the harmonies of acceptance, compassion, and kindness continue to echo through your life, guiding you toward a brighter, more loving future.

Remember, self-love is not a destination, but a journey. It's a continuous process of growth, learning, and evolution. May the 8 resonant notes of self-love be a constant reminder of your worth, your beauty, and your capacity to love yourself unconditionally.

As you close this book, I offer you a final thought: you are the conductor of your own life's symphony. You have the power to create harmony, to compose beauty, and to orchestrate love. May you continue to tune into the music of your soul, and may it guide you toward a life that is authentic, meaningful, and filled with love.

Thank you for joining me on this journey of self-love. May our paths cross again soon.

Love you all,

Piyush Singh

waiting for your feedback

psytedu24@gmail.com

Facebook Id- authorpiyush

Instagram Id- authorpiyush

Telegram Id- authorpiyush